THE COMPARISON GAME

STOP COMPARING YOURSELF TO
WHAT YOU SEE AND START BELIEVING
IN WHO GOD MADE YOU TO BE!

KIARRA NESBIT

THE COMPARISON GAME

Stop Comparing Yourself to What You See and Start Believing in Who God Made You to Be!

Copyright © 2024. Kiarra Nesbit. All rights reserved. No part of this publication may be reproduced, distributed, or transmitted in any form or by any means, including photocopying, recording, or other electronic or mechanical methods, without the prior written permission of the publisher, except in the case of brief quotations embodied in critical reviews and certain other noncommercial uses permitted by copyright law.

Edited by Mary Rembert
Cover design by Adeel A.
Interior design by Esther Moody

Scripture is taken from the New King James Version® unless otherwise noted.

ISBN: 979-8-9919295-0-9

"FOR GOD HAS NOT GIVEN US A SPIRIT OF FEAR, BUT OF POWER AND OF LOVE AND OF A SOUND MIND."

—2 TIMOTHY 1:7

CONTENTS

DEDICATION vii
INTRODUCTION ix
WHO THIS BOOK IS FOR xiii

CHAPTER 1. Where does it all begin? 1
CHAPTER 2. Overcoming Middle School! 15
CHAPTER 3. The Comparison Game:
High School 29
CHAPTER 4. Welcome to College! 43
CHAPTER 5. The Comparison Game:
Adult Life 57
CHAPTER 6. Social Media, Depression, & Suicide! 71
CHAPTER 7. After the storm comes the rainbow! 87
CHAPTER 8. The New Beginning...Comparing
Yourself to Jesus! 97

ACKNOWLEDGMENTS 113
ABOUT THE AUTHOR 115

DEDICATION

To my mother—who was there for me when I experienced the very first sign of rejection due to the way I looked, who believed in me when I was younger and told me I could be whatever I desired to be as long as I continued to put God first; the woman who reminded me of Psalm 23 when I was at my very lowest as a high school student; and the woman who still has a huge place in my heart. I thank you, and I love you.

INTRODUCTION

It was another endless night of tossing and turning, throwing my covers all over the place, my mind loudly telling me, *You're not enough; You will never be enough!* I can't hear anything but the yelling in my head. I crawl into a fetal position, but it doesn't ease the pain, so I go back to stretching out across the bed.

I try to speak, but no words are coming to me. I'm in complete darkness; I feel as though I'm beginning to sink into the bed from all the agony taking place around me.

Tears won't stop falling as the voices get louder and louder.
You will never have anything.
You are not beautiful.
No one will ever love you for you.
What are you doing with yourself?
You have already messed up too much for anyone to accept you.

I feel like screaming but can't because I'll wake my roommate. When will the voices stop? When will they leave me alone? When will the torment end? I have so much turmoil inside; I feel like I can't lift my head above water. I can't breathe. I am suffocating with my thoughts because I don't know who or why I am here.

My heart aches.
My head hurts.
I just want it to all go away.
I just want this pain to end.

God, where are you? Are you near to me? Do you see what I am going through? Do you care about me? Do you understand?

I feel very alone. I can't see myself out of this pain. There had been times when I would call on friends and get advice, but I couldn't even do that during this time. I didn't have the energy. The thoughts are rumbling and running rapidly in my head. I begin to hyperventilate as I try to calm myself down.

As if in answer, the Lord reminds me of the song "I'm in the midst of It All" by Fred Hammond. The song begins playing in my head as I cry out to God.

I sit up in bed, looking toward the wall. I close my eyes and begin to say the name of Jesus! I pace the floor and cry out his name over and over. I tell him I am scared, frustrated, angry, and anxious.

My chest won't stop racing. I am questioning if I will ever get to the point where I can just breathe and look at myself as worthy and valuable.

Will these voices cease? As I began to get the strength to call on the name of Jesus, I remind myself that I don't want to let myself go back to that scary dark space or throw in the towel and give up. These thoughts have tormented me for so many precious years. It has to stop, and I know I can't do it alone.

Finally, as I listen to the song's words and silence the noise of the enemy, ease begins to come upon me. The song ministers to my spirit, and I begin to sing the song to myself. God, you're in the midst of it all. You are here with me. You reminded me of this song for a reason.

At times, our mind races to the point where we feel there is no end. I am here to tell you that there is an end to the racing thoughts keeping you up at night, and it's literally falling in love with Jesus. If you have any negative thoughts regarding yourself or a circumstance, you will know how to fight it. Knowing who and whose you are stems from knowing your identity. When you know your identity and who it's in, there is no room for the comparison game to begin.

WHO THIS BOOK IS FOR

I wrote *The Comparison Game* because the Lord showed me that in today's society, so many of us get lost in the views and comments of life instead of understanding and knowing who we are without them.

Social media has played a huge part in explaining why many of us don't consider ourselves valuable or enough. Going through so much chaos regarding my looks in my earlier years took a toll on me internally in adulthood.

If you are struggling in this comparison game, I want to expose the enemy and his tricks so you, too, can be set free from the spirit of comparison, jealousy, envy, and pride and truly see yourself through the eyes of Our Father!

— CHAPTER 1 —

WHERE DOES IT ALL BEGIN?

> *"For I know the thoughts that I think toward you, says the Lord, thoughts of peace and not of evil, to give you a future and a hope."*
> —Jeremiah 29:11

Like most athletes, I loved to win. I never liked losing because it never felt good. When I won, it made me feel accomplished. A sense of satisfaction came over me when I got a victory over the other team. Whether it was in basketball, track, or cheerleading—you name it—I wanted the victory at the end.

But, there is one game that I unknowingly was playing for years and, unfortunately, was losing. What's the name of that game? It's called The Comparison Game.

The Comparison Game isn't fun. There are other opponents, but they are secret opponents because they don't know they are even in a game. After all, it's all going on in the player's head.

This game has two dealers, one good and the other evil. Which dealer will you listen to? One dealer's game will keep you up at night, having you question who you are and who's for you or against you. It'll have you fixated on the future rather than the present and, worst of all, not loving yourself.

The other dealer will have you understanding your true identity and fully loving yourself because you know who you are! So, who have you been listening to?

The Comparison Game can ruin your life—spiritually, mentally, physically, socially, and even financially. It can hinder you from moving toward what God wants to do in your life. There were many times when I would compare myself and forget the woman the Lord had called me to be! There were times when it would get me to the point of depression.

"Where is God?" I would ask myself. "**Doesn't he see me going through these trials? Doesn't He understand how much I am hurting?**"

Comparison can stifle your dreams and leave you feeling like time is running out. In reality, time isn't running out; comparing yourself makes you feel like it is. The Comparison Game is a game you must win every day of your life because when you are comparing yourself, you are downgrading yourself.

Okay, now it's time to get down to the nitty-gritty of things. Where does comparison all begin? Well, well, well, you may already know—**your mind!** The book *Deliverance From Demonic Covenants and Curses,* by Rev. James A. Solomon, states that satan starts planting negative seeds in our heads early on in life.

Let's think of a flower. Flowers are extremely beautiful yet peaceful, and they all come from seeds. According to an article on betterhomesandgarden.com,[1] there are many steps to ensure a seed is planted properly. First, you must find the right spot to plant. Some flowers need sun, and some need

---

1   Lucy Fitzgerald, "How to Grow Plants from Succulent Seeds," Better Homes & Gardens, March 7, 2023, https://www.bhg.com/gardening/flowers/perennials/growing-succulents-from-seeds/.

shade. Next, if you want your flower to grow in a healthy (righteous) way, you must find the right soil. According to Webster's Dictionary, soil is firm land, the upper layer of the earth that may be dug or plowed and where plants grow. It is the superficial, unconsolidated, and usually weathered part of the earth's mantle.

TRUTH MOMENT #1:

There is so much revelation in the definition of soil! Ahhhh! Soil provides the foundation for the flower to grow strong and mighty. So, as you are building your firm foundation in the Lord (good seeds), you will begin to grow strong, mighty, and courageous. No matter what may come your way, if your foundation is the Word of God, you can blossom. Yes, it may not look like anything is happening right now, but trust the process!

Once you have soil, you must select the location for your flower to grow. You must find the right location for the seed to be planted. If it isn't in the right location, your flower won't grow properly. Remember, some flowers need sunlight, and some need shade. When it is the right time, you must plant the seed 1/4 inch deep (that's not really that deep, right?). After planting the seed, you must cover, fertilize, and water it.

Now, where am I going with this? You must understand the trick of the enemy when it comes to you. The enemy has evil seeds that he plants in your good soil, aka your mind—which, at one time, was free from any chaos, turmoil, or baggage. He's there to kill, steal, and destroy you in ANY WAY he can! Trust me. So, yes, while you are growing into this beautiful flower, "be sober, be vigilant, because your adversary the devil walks about like a roaring lion, seeking whom he may devour" (1 Peter 5:8). He is literally planting, fertilizing, and watering seeds in every phase of your life, and he starts when you're young.

SOME SEEDS STEAL YOUR IDENTITY

If you grew up like I did, you had both parents in the house. I had a father and mother who loved me dearly. Everything was great, but then I found out that the man who raised me wasn't my biological father.

One afternoon at my grandfather's house, I remember talking to my mother and asking her if I could call my biological father and let him know that I knew that he was my father.

As I picked up the phone and dialed the number, I was extremely nervous. Not knowing what kind of response I would get from him was nerve-racking.

My stomach was in knots as the phone started ringing. Finally, catching the voice on the end of the phone, I was super excited to say what I knew, but I realized that it wouldn't matter.

Hearing the words, "I'm not your father," and being denied by him when we both knew he was lying was heartbreaking. I hung up the phone and cried uncontrollably. I hurt in a way that I didn't even think I could.

As I think back on this story, I remember wondering what had happened to have him hang up on me and talk to me the way he did. In my mind, it made me wonder what made my biological father disown me.

The why doesn't matter at this point. What matters most is that I now had to understand that my Father in heaven sent me a father on earth to love and cherish me. Even though

I knew this, it didn't negate my feelings! Deep down, I still wondered and questioned what had happened.

This was a trick from the enemy to plant seeds in my head as a young girl. The enemy then began to water the seed with doubt, anger, depression, anxiety, and even fear from his tricks and schemes. This led to many things happening throughout my life, such as believing lies about myself, feeling less than others, and even experiencing strife between those in my household. Crazy, right?

As you can see, the devil begins to plant and water seeds early by allowing things to happen through other people—sometimes the people you love. Now, do the people saying and doing things know what's happening? Some do, but many don't know that the seeds they've planted in your mind will follow you into adulthood and, sometimes, have irreversible effects.

According to *NBC15 News*, more than 50,000 Americans committed suicide in 2023.[2] When that comes to mind, it is so powerful. We must know how to silence the voices before the enemy's seeds destroy everything.

TRUTH MOMENT #2:

If you grew up without a father in your life or your biological father is not around, let me say this very clearly for you: **You have a father in heaven that loves and adores you so much! He knows your every need before you even speak it out. Mkay!** Our amazing Father in Heaven sent me an

---

2 Karris Harmon, "Suicide Rates for 2023 at an All-Time High for the United States," WPMI, January 3, 2024, https://mynbc15.com/news/nation-world/suicide-rates-for-2023-at-an-all-time-high-for-the-united-states.

amazing man who raised me to be the woman I am today! I am so grateful for his heart toward me because even though I wasn't his, he took me under his wing as if I were his biological daughter!

Now that I am older and understand more about what goes on in the spiritual realm, I can identify how the enemy was watering his seeds in elementary school. I can remember it like it was yesterday, from being bullied by five girls in the bathroom to having my Ricky Martin lunch box thrown in the toilet. Yes, I loved Ricky Martin growing up! Livin' la vida loca, baby!

I transferred schools and thought it would be over. It wasn't. Going from physical to verbal bullying didn't change anything. Being a very petite girl in elementary school drew a lot of negativity my way. I went through so much when it came to my skin complexion and my size. One of the things that stuck with me for years, even into adulthood, was being called "toothpick."

The saying goes, "Sticks and stones may break your bones, but words can never hurt you." Let's just say words can definitely hurt. They can cut deep and stay there for years. That is until one decides enough is enough and begins doing the work to release all the negativity that has been sitting within. The fact that I was a crybaby didn't make those years any better! But all I knew was that what people were doing to me really hurt me in a way you can't imagine.

TRUTH MOMENT #3:

I was a softy, but I am here to let you know that **it is okay to be in tune with your emotions. Just don't let them overtake** you. Some people are not so in tune with their emotions, and they wish they were. If you feel like crying because you have been hurt, then CRY! Do not hold your tears in. Trust me, there is someone near who is ready to catch every drop that falls down your face. Who is that someone? Jesus Christ!

After elementary school, I thought it would get better. Can I say it definitely wasn't better?! At first, I thought that I could get along with everyone. It was a new school, new people, new environment—so what could possibly go wrong?

Well, the seeds followed me to middle school. Yes, the people in my grade were the same as before, but now there were new upper-class students I could potentially get along with. I cultivated friendships with people a little older than me, which led to constantly feeling like I was less than and not good enough to be around certain people.

I often wonder why I was always a target. Both men and women would do and say certain things to get under my skin. Did it sit well with me? No! Many times, I would allow it to happen without saying anything back because I was afraid. Fear would creep up on me because I didn't want to get into a fight. I would try to just keep the peace.

Keeping the peace was also a huge thing for me in high school. For one, it was a way to avoid altercations. I would allow people to say things to me without standing up for myself. What was the verbal bullying doing to me, though? Planting seeds! The enemy knew who to allow to say things, let alone do things.

If I can tell you anything right now, **please stand up for yourself**. Raise your voice, and let it be heard! Now, I do not condone fighting, but at least do not allow yourself to get bullied and pushed around. You are capable and able to stand up for yourself.

As you get older, you'll understand why some, if not most, people would do bad things. Either they have things going on at home or are dealing with things internally and want to take it out on whoever they can.

We will dig deeper into fear in another chapter because even as I write this portion of the book, I realize that I was letting fear run my life! I now know I have the power and authority to shut fear up and move on from what has hindered me for years! As it says in 2 Timothy 1:7, "For God has not given us a spirit of fear, but of power and of love and of a sound mind."

TIME OF REFLECTION!

(Grab your tea, coffee, bottled water, and a pen and journal, sister!)

1. Can you remember a time that you believe the enemy began to plant seeds in your life? If so, when? How were you feeling then?
2. Are any negative seeds from your childhood still with you today?
3. Do you believe you can be free from the tricks of the enemy and begin to live a life that isn't filled by comparing yourself to those around you? (**It's okay to be honest with yourself. That's where the healing truly begins.**)

THE COMPARISON GAME

THE COMPARISON GAME | 11

— CHAPTER 2 —

OVERCOMING MIDDLE SCHOOL

"For do I now persuade men, or God? Or do I seek to please men? For if I still pleased men, I would not be a bondservant of Christ."
—Galatians 1:10

Middle school was fun for the most part! I was in cheerleading, going to school dances, beta club conventions, and so many other things. I thought these experiences would make life less painful, but in all reality, they didn't.

Let's go back to fifth grade for a second. Remember the name "toothpick"? Well, going into middle school, the bullying started to happen more frequently regarding how small I was. I began to think that there was something really wrong with me. So, one day, I went home and talked to my mom about it. I remember telling her about the things people would say to me regarding my skin complexion and my size.

"Is there something wrong with me?" I asked her.

"There is absolutely nothing wrong with you," my mom replied. "Do you want to know why? Well, it's because God created you, and you are His! You are fearfully and wonderfully made in His image."

I remember thinking differently to myself.

"Why are people picking on me then? Will this ever stop? Am I too skinny?"

See, even though my mother told me the truth, my mind spoke the opposite. I honestly wanted to grasp what my mother said the Lord said. I wanted to believe that the fact that the Lord created me meant that I didn't have to worry about what anyone else said. Well, that didn't happen.

Instead, the thoughts that I had during that time sounded like:

Should I wear something different?

Maybe I could've stood up for myself.

Did I do anything wrong in the beginning besides being myself?

Why am I even here?

Do I just need to try to be friends with the people bullying me anyway?

Will this ever stop?

Have you ever thought like this? Have you ever felt that something was wrong with you because of the opinions of others? Have you felt you need to try to please others so their negative opinions of you would stop? If so, let me tell you, *there is absolutely nothing wrong with you!* I don't care what people have been saying to or about you. God knew exactly why he wanted you to look the way you do and be the way you are.

Now, if you don't have anyone encouraging you or who can be there for you when you need them, I am here to tell you that you are created and formed the way the Lord wanted you to be formed (Isaiah 43: 1-2).

Everything about you is good in God's eyes—the way your hair and eyes are, the color of your skin, and even how your body is shaped. Whether you are slim-figured or a woman with curves, you are enough, and you are worthy.

If you aren't a believer in the Lord and Savior Jesus Christ, I will tell you this (and I hope it sits with you): Get to know him for yourself, and learn what he says about you. You are fearfully and wonderfully made by our Father in Heaven who created us (Psalm 139:14). No atom or big bang created us as humans. Jesus Christ did! Point blank, period.

Now, about these classmates of mine, was it cool that they were picking on me? Absolutely not. Did I think it was my fault that they were picking on me? I did. If you think being bullied is your fault, then I am here to share with you that it is not. You can't help that some people have personal things going on and haven't sat with themselves and gotten down to the nitty-gritty of things. They take whatever they're dealing with out on others they perceive as weaker to make themselves feel better!

Let's make this clear: **you are not weak.**

Standing up for yourself is important because it shows people you aren't inferior to anyone. As it says in Deuteronomy 31:6, "Be strong and of good courage, do not fear nor be afraid of them; for the Lord your God, He is the One who goes with you. He will not leave you nor forsake you."

As you reread that scripture, let it take root in your mind. Be strong. That means when you feel weak, call upon the Lord, and He will be your strength during any trouble. Your strength comes from the Lord. Humans can be physically strong, but when it comes to being spiritually strong, we must rely on the Lord.

As it states in 2 Corinthians 12:9-10, "And He said to me, 'My grace is sufficient for you, for My strength is made perfect in weakness.' Therefore, most gladly I will rather boast in my infirmities, that the power of Christ may rest upon me. Therefore I take pleasure in infirmities, in reproaches, in needs, in persecutions, in distresses, for Christ's sake. For when I am weak, then I am strong."

So, the next time the spirit of intimidation arises, you speak against it and stand up for yourself against the enemy. You let him know that you are not fighting this battle by yourself, but God in Heaven is fighting this battle with you. Call on Jehovah Gibbor, who is Mighty in Battle and ready to go to war with you.

What if you are afraid of them?
What are some things that you are afraid of? Is it failing, animals, or maybe the dark? In middle school, I was afraid of all three, but I was also scared of the opinions of the people I would see daily. This began to mess with my identity. Are we supposed to fear people and what they could do to us? Absolutely not. We shouldn't fear anyone who could harm the body, but not the soul. Rather, fear the one who can harm both the body and the soul (Matthew 10:28). Who am I referencing? Our Lord and Savior Jesus Christ!

What does this have to do with comparison?
Whether you have experienced physical bullying, verbal bullying, spiritual bullying, or even cyberbullying, each of these can have a significant impact on how you view yourself as a person compared to others. It's like a piece of you is stolen—well, this is what I felt like. I remember times in middle school when things said to me weren't so nice: things concerning my size and skin color. It made me question who

I was and wonder why it was happening to me. They were saying things that took root, and even though I grew up in church, I didn't know how to fight them. Did I know at the time that it would affect me so much? No, I didn't, but now, as an adult, I see how to fight differently.

If you don't know how to fight, be intentional about grabbing your Bible and reading about fighting with the sword of the spirit (Ephesians 6:17), which is the Word of God. The enemy can and will try to throw seeds at your mind, but you will have your weapon and know how to fight! In a later chapter, I will discuss how the enemy's tactics affected my adulthood. Whew, get ready!

Now, what about your friends?
We will discuss this topic throughout the entire book because, as it says in the Word, "A man who has friends must himself be friendly, but there is a friend who sticks closer than a brother" (Proverbs 18:24). I thought that my friends would stick close, but we all know that there are times when that can change.

For a while, I didn't understand the true meaning of friendship because I was bullied by some of my friends, but friendship was still very important to me and my walk with Christ. There was something about being able to have someone the same age to do life with.

Even Jesus had friends (the disciples) with whom He walked this earth, and He cared so much for people. Back then, I desired friendship a lot. I was the type of girl who wanted everyone to like her. I wanted to fit in! Little did I know my closest friends would plant some of the most hurtful seeds. There was someone whom I considered an extremely close person in my life. It's like we understood each other until she started to bully me. I never knew the underlying issue until later. Now, I will not disclose what I was told as to why she came to school to bully me, but I am here to tell you that *it is never you!*

There is absolutely nothing wrong with you, but I want to let you know one thing: you are not meant to fit in; you are meant to stand out. Yes, things may happen to you, but you will think from a VICTOR mindset!

Standing out means you may not do what everyone else does. You may prefer to wear different things than everyone else likes to wear. You may not listen to the same music as they do. You may not play the same sports or even like sports. But you are you, unapologetically. Never, I mean never, apologize for being yourself like I did. I apologized for being who I was instead of just being me and loving every part of me. I even apologized for crying! I really was a people-pleaser at heart.

Whew, did I just say that?

Yes, I did.

I tried to please everyone around me because I just wanted to be liked. I didn't care what someone had done to me. I just wanted everyone and everything to be easy peasy, lemon squeezy! Being kind is what I thought would change the way people treated me.

It is one of the fruits of the spirit (Galatians 5:22-23), along with love, joy, peace, longsuffering, goodness, faithfulness, gentleness, and self-control. We are to be kind to one another, but be careful not to confuse it with being too nice.

According to Webster's Dictionary, nice is defined as being pleasing and agreeable. But kind is defined as a sympathetic or helpful nature. Regarding how people speak to you and how they carry on regarding you, you should be kind to them but never overly nice. You know the old saying, "Kill them with kindness." That's what you do. Growing up, I knew nothing about this; I thought I had to take what everyone was dishing out toward me, but you don't have to do that.

Let's just say that being a people-pleaser will get old and wear you out quickly if you let it. We are not here to please man but to please the one and only person who has our best interest at heart, no matter what we do!

Trust me, you may have someone right now bullying and threatening you into doing all of their work. Let me tell you one thing—vengeance is the Lord's, it is not yours (Romans 12:19). So, if they want to be that way and post something about you or even try to put their hands on you, don't worry. Remember that God is fighting your battle!

Thinking back on those years, all I can say is that I wish I knew then what I know now. Many things can occur in middle school, but I am here to tell you to fight. Fight spiritually, though, not physically! "For we do not wrestle against flesh and blood, but against principalities, against powers, against the rulers of the darkness of this age, against spiritual hosts of wickedness in the heavenly places"(Ephesians 6:12). You have what it takes to overcome every obstacle thrown at you. Fight back with the word and trust that God has your back.

TIME OF REFLECTION!

(Grab your tea, coffee, bottled water, and a pen and journal, sister!)

1. How are you managing the thoughts running throughout your mind during the day? Are you allowing them to overtake what you know is true, or are you allowing them to run around in your mind fully?!
2. Some thoughts are not your thoughts. These thoughts belong to someone else and not you. When they get to the point of being too much to handle, what do you resort to?
3. Where did these thoughts begin in the first place?
4. If you were bullied, how did it make you feel? What were the thoughts that came to mind as it was happening?
5. Are you a people-pleaser?

24 | KIARRA NESBIT

THE COMPARISON GAME

KIARRA NESBIT

—CHAPTER 3—
THE COMPARISON GAME: HIGH SCHOOL

"For you formed my inward parts; You covered me in my mother's womb. I will praise You, for I am fearfully and wonderfully made; Marvelous are Your works, And that my soul knows very well."
—Psalm 139:13-14

Okay, here come the "best" years of your life—high school, woohoo! By this time, I was older, a little wiser, and more confident in myself. I thought I wouldn't let people run over me with their comments and opinions. What could go wrong? Well, comparison seeds had followed me into high school!

I was constantly thinking things like:

You will never be good enough.
You might as well kill yourself because no one likes you.
You aren't beautiful.
You're too dark.
You're too skinny.
You have no real friends.
You should just run away.

The list went on and on! Sometimes, the thoughts would get so loud that I couldn't hear God's voice over the enemy's. There were even times I would believe the thoughts even though I knew they weren't true. Was it tough not to believe these thoughts? Yes.

See, here is the thing. Once the enemy knows he can get to you through your thoughts, he no longer has to come at you any other way. He knows all he has to do is throw the same scenario your way, using the same or similar people, to keep you going in the same cycle. Let's just say cycles are no fun! You can go through them for years and years if you do not get a grip on yourself.

What makes a cycle a cycle? Let me show you an example. Constantly doing the same repetitive thing over and over again, thinking you will get a different result. In reality, if you are doing the same thing repeatedly, you will get the same result.

To get a different result, you must do something different! Let's say you didn't make the cheerleading team like you wanted to. Each year, you tried out but didn't practice, put forth the effort to learn something new, and so on, so you didn't make it. If you want to see a different result with cheerleading, you must put forth the effort to practice.

This is with everything in life, though! Whatever you want to do in life, you **must** put forth effort to learn about whatever you are intrigued about. So, if you don't grab hold of the cycle, thoughts will begin to arise, and you may even start thinking negatively about yourself.

Now, every time an opportunity comes up, you doubt yourself and don't put forth the effort to see if you can accomplish what you really want to do. The enemy now doesn't have to come and bother you because you will cancel yourself out before he even has to.

If you are doing this today, please stop! Even if you didn't make the team, didn't get a good grade, or didn't win homecoming and your friend did—that doesn't mean you aren't good enough. You are good enough!

Even though I was extremely positive, the negative thoughts got louder and louder throughout high school.

"You're too dark."

Remember the opinions about me being too dark in middle school? Well, it was still a thought in my head in high school. Some people can brush things off, but I just couldn't release my feelings for some reason! I felt like a victim instead of a victor. It hindered me from moving forward and had me wondering if there would ever be people who genuinely liked or loved me.

It made me question everyone in my life—even myself. I mean, having a victim mentality is never good. When things happen to you, you may become a victim, but you don't have to remain one. If you do, it won't do anything to the other person but will do more to you.

"You should just run away."

Have you ever considered quitting school because of the circumstances you faced? Well, I did. There were many times I wanted to run away, but I couldn't. Many people consider high school years something to remember, but I was just waiting for graduation!

Do you currently want to run away? Why? Will that solve all your problems? No, running never solves anything. (That's in ALL areas of your life.) You must meet whatever circumstance that you're facing head-on. Now, will this be scary? Absolutely!

"You have no real friends."

Have there been times when you felt as though everyone around you was out to get you due to bullying? Did it make you feel alone and afraid? There have been many times when I would feel this way. Even though people were around me and I knew I had friends, I would still feel lonely! Being on the bus full of people, talking, laughing, and still feeling alone internally. Fighting back the tears, fighting back the loud noise in your head.

Why was this, do you think? Well, if you aren't strong enough to silence the thoughts in your mind, you will begin to believe there is no one for you! These are lies that the enemy is telling you. "Be sober, be vigilant, because your adversary the devil walks about like a roaring lion, seeking whom he may devour" *(1 Peter 5:8)*. The enemy comes to steal, kill, and destroy *(John 10:10)* any little thing that you could even think you are capable of doing, achieving, or having.

When I was a teen, the Word wasn't always the first thing that came to mind. I thought about more practical things, such as, "If I just change classes, I will be okay." Or "If I just switch schools again, that will work" (even though you already did that). Or, "If I hide and wait until they leave, all will be well."

Well, none of those will work. You must be willing to stand still and seek God to make the right decision in what to do. Understand that you are more than a conqueror (according to Romans 8:37), and God is with you everywhere you go! Do you know that?

"You aren't beautiful."

Okay, now on to this thought that constantly arose in my head daily. Let's talk about the "You aren't beautiful" lie. Well, well, well, I will come to you all and say that you are beautiful! You are fearfully and wonderfully made by our Father in heaven *(Psalm 139:14)*.

Did it take me a while to understand this for myself? Yes. Even as I type this now, I am still growing through this. I am still understanding my true beauty. As I sip my water typing this, I embrace my natural curly hair with no nails! Ahhh, is that me? Well, yes, it is! I am literally embracing all of me as I type this book.

The Lord laid it on my heart and gave me a dream of taking out my braids to embrace everything else about me—curls and all. Now, has this taken some getting used to? Yes, ma'am, it has. In high school, I would have never gone out with just my natural curl pattern without trying to stretch my hair. Honestly, I didn't know how to do that well, lol.

Anywho, beauty goes beyond the outer appearance. Yes, we have things that can enhance our beauty, like makeup, extensions, eyelashes, acrylic nails, and even stylish clothing; I mean, you name it. Though you don't need any of this, you're beautiful just the way you are.) But beauty is what's within. What does your heart look like? Are you that girl who constantly celebrates others' successes, or do you envy them deep down because you wish it were you? Be real with yourself. I know I had to.

Once a seed is planted, you must work to overcome what the enemy is trying to tell you, which is a lie!

One thing the enemy is after is your mind, a powerful thing given to you by your Father in Heaven. Remember that as you go through your life. If the enemy can come to interrupt your thoughts with negative seeds, he has you—and everything concerning you—in the palm of his hands.

Make up your mind that you will not let the enemy do this to you again, and that is when you can begin to do the work that needs to be done! There are many things that the enemy will try to throw your way, but you must be strong and courageous and fight those thoughts.

There are many scriptures that I have come across over the years to help me fight, but there is one that I still, to this day, recite because the enemy isn't giving up, and neither am I. The scripture is 2 Corinthians 10: 4-6, and it states, "For the weapons of our warfare are not carnal but mighty in God for pulling down strongholds, casting down arguments and every high thing that exalts itself against the knowledge of God, bringing every thought into captivity to the obedience of Christ, and being ready to punish all disobedience when your obedience is fulfilled."

NEGATIVE THOUGHTS AND COMPARISON

Are you someone who constantly compares yourself to someone else? Are you comparing your looks or maybe even your size? Well, let's stop here! I know that society may say that you have to look this way or appear to be like this, but I want to tell you whether you're Black (light or dark), White, Asian, Indian, Hispanic, or any other race not named here, you should never compare yourself to others.

I'm going to say this again: you should never compare yourself to anyone else other than the person you see in the mirror. .

Really look at yourself. How do you see yourself now versus how you want to see yourself in the future? Always remember that looking at yourself and becoming whole in who you are—and not wondering about who you are not—is extremely important in your ability not to compare yourself. Whew, I had to tell myself that even as I began to write this book.

On a side note, I was still growing in this area at the beginning of this journey in writing *The Comparison Game*. See, you're not in this alone! Trust me, I get it. There were moments when I would compare myself to things around me. I am just being honest here. Comparing my journey, my looks, my hair, my money, and how my walk with Christ looked compared to others—I mean, you name it.

What did that do, though? It hindered me from accomplishing so much in my life. To this day, I believe and know I should've been so much further than I currently am. But hey, it's okay. Do you know why? God hasn't given up on me, and He isn't going to give up on you!

TIME OF REFLECTION!

(Grab your tea, coffee, bottled water, and a pen and journal, sister!)

1. What were the things you endured throughout high school that made you question yourself?
2. Do you truly believe that the Lord created you in His image and that you are fearfully and wonderfully made?
3. Who are some people that you compare yourself to? What can you learn from the Lord's Word to help you triumph over the thoughts in your mind?

THE COMPARISON GAME

THE COMPARISON GAME | 41

— CHAPTER 4 —

WELCOME TO COLLEGE

> "Examine yourselves as to whether you are in the faith. Test yourselves, that Jesus Christ is in you? Unless indeed you are disqualified."
> —2 Corinthians 13:5

Oh, the college days! For those who are in college now, live it up. **But, know who you are and whose you are, mkay**! In my opinion, your college years are your defining years. Yes, you may be fresh out of your parent's home or still in their house.

Either way, these are the years where you get to decide who YOU want to be—not what someone else wants you to be, not what you think APPEARS to be a cool career title, but who it is the Father has called you to be.

Let's talk about your career for a moment. When it comes to the career that you want to do, ask yourself this... Why am I wanting to do this career? Is it to please men? Is it because I desire to? Is it because the Lord has told me to? What is the reason? If you don't know why you are wanting to step into the career that is before you, I advise you to sit with the Lord, and get the blueprint from heaven on what you should do.

As a young adult in college, there are some things you need to understand about the spiritual world. **It is real, and a real battle is going on for your soul.** Now, am I trying to scare you? No, I am not, I am just letting you know that this is a real thing. There is a real enemy out there, and it's the devil. He wants to distract you and get you to compare what God is doing or even wants to do in your life.

If you have a hard time hearing the Lord and understanding his voice, there are practical ways of learning how to hear the voice of the Lord. Some ways are through creation, fasting, adoration, meditation, solitude, learning, movement, and even conversation. I am only telling you this because even though I grew up in the church, there were many things that I had to unlearn and learn again to have a personal relationship with the Father and hear from Him. Would I say I could hear the Father clearly during my college years? Not really no, because I began to listen to the world more than listen to the voice of the Lord.

When I sit to think about my college years, I would definitely say I was lukewarm because I still did what I wanted to do, barely prayed, and wasn't in my word like I was supposed to be. I was wearing the cross around my neck, but was I dying to myself in these years? No. I would appear as a believer on the outside, and I desired to be like Christ, but I also wanted things to go the way I wanted them to. My college years opened me up to a lot I wasn't ready for internally.

So, to save you some heartache and time, please understand who you are in the Lord, take up your cross daily, and follow Him. Get in the Word because it will help you through the tough times. You are who you are for a reason, but invite God in so that he can help you understand who you are in Him!

So, on another note college was some of my most fun yet life-changing years. I was out in the real world, trying to understand life on my own without my parents around. Mind you, I would still contact my parents to ask them if I could go out to a club. What in the world? Yes, remember I said, "Lukewarm." Whew, I would proclaim Christ but still be in atmospheres that the Lord didn't want me in!

Walking the campus and feeling free without a care in the world, I began to see life differently. It was a new set of people, new scenery, and I was starting to feel like I could breathe (because, honey, high school was suffocating)! Meeting new friends and teachers, I said, "Okay, I can do this college life." But then, it was like the enemy already had things lined up for me. As a dear friend of mine this day would say, "Just as God has the play-by-play for my life, the enemy does too. The thing is, though, he has no power!"

Let me say that again: **The enemy has no power!** He only has power if we give it to him.

Throughout college, I would go to clubs, drink, smoke hookah, and feel so out of place at times. I wonder why?!? Well, you know why! The Holy Spirit began to help me understand that this is not the lifestyle that the Lord has for me.

On top of that, I wouldn't get the male attention I wanted. I am being honest because it's where more negative seeds began to get planted! My sisters, let me tell you something right now: "Please do not worry if you do not get the attention you want from a man. The only attention you should want is from Our Father in heaven and the man He sends your way." Mkay!

Even though I experienced this, there were still many occasions where I wanted to be in the spotlight. I thought I needed to be in the spotlight to get the attention I wanted. Let me just say, this is a dangerous place to be! Wanting to be in the spotlight to get attention is not from the Lord. It is not about you.

Growing up, I was always in the spotlight, and I believed that was how my life was supposed to go. From being in pageants to homecoming court to everyone knowing me because of the sports I played, I thought my entire life had to be on display. Well, I am here to tell you, whether you're in the spotlight or not, **focus on the lord because He is the spotlight.** Don't do anything for self-gain. If you do, you will not get anything out of that. You may get the accolades and the nice things in life, but it could leave you so empty inside.

Nevertheless, not knowing, this made me began to compare myself even more. I was looking at other women around me who were getting chosen and did not understand why I wasn't. I started wanting to eat more to gain weight and be seen. I was trying to fit in where I knew I wasn't meant to fit in and began to try to change my outer appearance just to feel seen.

I mean, ladies you MUST check your motives as to WHY you are doing certain things in the first place. Now that I see what I was doing, I can share that you don't have to pretend to be someone you aren't.

I had no clue about the devil's tactics back then. I would let thoughts run rampant in my mind regarding how I looked daily! I spent more time in the mirror wondering if my outfit and hair looked okay than anything else—all because I wanted the attention I thought I was missing out on. If this is happening in your life, repeat after me: "Devil, I am privy to your tactics, and I am NOT giving up on what the Lord said. You will not have me or my mind!"

Here are 7 practical things you can do now that you are aware of his schemes, but you must be willing to turn from your way to truly follow Christ.

PRACTICAL THINGS YOU CAN DO:

- **Pray.**
- Put on the whole Armour of God **daily**. (Ephesians 6:14-17)
- Remind yourself of who God says you are.
- Find scripture to fight against the lies of the enemy.
- Worship the Father in Spirit and in Truth. (John 4:23-24)
- Give the Holy Spirit room to allow Jesus more and more into your life.
- **Decrease** and let the Father **increase**. (John 3:30)

Was I thinking any of that when I was in college? No, I wasn't. I thought just going to church every Sunday and spending a little time with Him here and there would be okay. You must cultivate a true, intimate relationship with The Father to understand what He desires for you to do with your life.

COMPARISON IN THE BIBLE

While spending time in the Word, I realized many stories dealt with comparison and competition! One in particular is the story of Rachael and Leah in Genesis 29.

Now, Rachael and Leah were daughters of Laban, Jacob's uncle. Rachael was the youngest daughter and Leah was the oldest. Jacob loved Rachael. There was so much competition between the two sisters because of the way life happened for them both. Leah was the sister who was fertile and could have children for Jacob, while Rachael was the sister that received the attention from Jacob.

Jacob fell in love with Rachel the very first moment he saw her. Jacob worked for seven years just to marry Rachel, a woman he met once. Okay, we see that Rachel is the woman Jacob is madly in love with, but he is deceived, by his uncle, into marrying Leah.

So, Laban told him to complete that first week of the wedding; then he would give him Rachel in return for working for him for another seven years! The thing is, he did just that. He literally began working for Laban for another seven years just to marry Rachel. If you'd like to dig deeper into this story, I would encourage you to! It's very eye opening.

So, why bring up this story? Well, to show you that comparison didn't start with you. Comparison has been around since the beginning of time. Sometimes we think that we are the only ones that are going through something, and in reality we are not the only ones.

There were many times during my college years where I literally would think I was the only one going through a problem. It's crazy because as I sit and think about this, I would magnify the problem instead of understanding who has the solution to my problem. It is so important to not magnify the problem, because magnifying the problem won't add anything to your life. Is this tough to do at times? Yes, but you can do it. Take some time to meditate on Matthew 6:27.

Also, these were the years where I believe that I began to really worry about the opinions of others little by little. This is a dangerous place to be. Worrying about the opinions of others will really get you in a place of stopping instead of going.

Now what do I mean by that? There could be something that you are supposed to be doing with your life, but because you worry about what others would say, you begin to hinder yourself from the opportunities that may come your way without even noticing it. I've done this so much honestly. I am here to tell you that the opinions of others really do not matter. What only matters is what God says about you. You may hear this a lot throughtout the book. I am here to just let you know that this is a trick of the enemy to have you worrying about what others may say or feel about you. Please don't get stuck there.

Even though I experienced this, there were many occasions when I wanted to be in the spotlight. I thought I needed to be in the spotlight to get the attention I wanted. Let me just say, this is a dangerous place to be! Wanting to be in the spotlight to get attention is not of God. It is not about you!

Growing up, I was always in the spotlight, and I believed that was how my life was supposed to go. From being in pageants to homecoming court to everyone knowing me because of the sports I played, I thought my entire life had to be on display. Well, I am here to tell you, whether you're in the spotlight or not, **focus on the Lord because He is the spotlight.** Don't do anything for self-gain. If you do, you will not get anything out of that! You may get the accolades and the nice things in life, but you could be so empty inside.

The Lord sees you and He loves you so much! You will be reminded of this throughout this entire book because it is so true. The Lord sees everything you do. He understands every little detail about you. If you haven't made it to college yet, in college now, or may even be out of college, remain true to yourself, understand the authority you have in Jesus, and put your complete faith in Him!

TIME OF REFLECTION!

(Grab your tea, coffee, bottled water, and a pen and journal, sister!)

1. What are some things you can begin to declare over yourself right now that you will carry on with you through your college years? If you've already graduated, what things did you wish you'd declared over yourself?
2. What are some things that you would tell your younger self?
3. How important to you is your career? If God told you to do something else, would you?
4. What is the main goal that you have for yourself concerning your walk with Christ?

THE COMPARISON GAME | 51

52 | KIARRA NESBIT

THE COMPARISON GAME

THE COMPARISON GAME

— CHAPTER 5 —

THE COMPARISON GAME: ADULT LIFE

> "Finally, brethren, whatever things are true, whatever things are noble, whatever things are just, whatever things are pure, whatever things are lovely, whatever things are of good report, if there is any virtue and if there is anything praiseworthy—meditate on these things."
> —Philippians 4:8

No more college?! Okay! Now it's time to step into the real world and pull up your big girl pants! Entering into the world as an adult is whatever you make of it.

But if you haven't dealt with the trauma from your college days or earlier, well, let's just say you may experience some of the same cycles throughout your adulthood.

Now, as for me, the negative thoughts got louder, especially regarding my love life. They reached the point where I was beginning to believe every thought coming to me. This was one area where I wasn't seeing the Lord move.

Because of the unresolved wounds from my past, the things that were told to me began crippling my life. Honestly speaking, if you do not do the necessary work to heal from your past, you will see yourself going into this repetitive cycle that gets aggravating.

The thing is, even though I was so aggravated by it, it still took me a long time to grasp what God was saying about me. As you try to grow and mature in your walk with Christ, the enemy will come at you really hard. He will continue to jab and jab at you until he has gotten you right where he wants you. When he knows he's gotten you, he will play baseball with your mind until he gets a home run. This means he will continue to throw these thoughts in your mind, which will have you running around and around and back and forth regarding any situation.

Once he makes a home run (which is having you spiraling over a situation), he moves into the second round, which will begin to have you questioning everything around you! Those negative seeds you don't deal with can begin to form a root in your adult life.

Let's dig a little deeper. As an adult, many responsibilities arise. These can include financial problems, health issues, living arrangements, car trouble, career shifts, children, marriage—you name it.

Could these things happen while we are in high school? Why yes, they can. But they aren't as maximized as they are when we become adults in my opinion. As the stresses of life weigh in, you must deal with them head-on. There is absolutely **no running away** from what you need to address.

When you begin to feel the weight of everything, don't give up. I know sometimes giving up seems easier, but that is not the answer. We are going to talk about that in the next chapter.

You must fight the good fight of faith and know you are not the only one fighting on your behalf. Jesus is also fighting with you and praying that you do not give in to the enemy's tricks to make you feel like your life is worse than everyone else's! Like the Lord said in Luke 22:31-34, "... Simon, Simon! Indeed, Satan has asked for you, that he may sift you as wheat. But I have prayed for you, that your faith should not fail; and when you have returned to Me, strengthen your brethren."

Jesus is praying that your faith does not fail or waiver when the weight of the world becomes heavy.

As I was writing this chapter, I began to love all of me. Was it easy to get to this point? No. Comparison used to sneak up in the simplest things, even though I thought I had dealt with the issue.

You must, I repeat, *you must* sit down with yourself in your early years to get to the root of your comparison so it won't show up in your future!

So, when it comes to comparison, I will say it lingered in my adult life for years. Things were said to me regarding my walk with Christ and whether I really knew his word. I mean, sheesh. Who would've thought that would have been thrown at me as a joke? Not only was I dealing with not loving myself, but also comparing my walk with Christ to others around me based on a few statements here and there.

I began to ask the Lord, "Now, God, where in my life do I need to grow?" I had to have tough conversations with myself because if others were seeing something, then what was I missing?

I am here to tell you **we will forever be students of the Lord.** Looking back on where I was to where I am now, there are things that you MUST do so you can be stronger in Him and not allow the things (and people) of this world to sway you left and right! No more swaying! Remain on the boat with the Father and let him guide you, OKAY?

There are many things we can compare ourselves to in adulthood. Not only physically or spiritually but also financially, lifestyle, and professionally—everything that is important to us as adults.

The thing I want you to remember, though, is it's never the person that you have the issue with or you're comparing yourself with. This thing is spiritual. It's a spiritual fight *every single day*. The enemy doesn't want you to be great, so he will make you think that it's you who doesn't like the way you look or the way you're living.

It's a mindset. If there is something you want to change or work on, just do it. That's what I had to tell myself numerous times. There were times when I began to compare myself, especially if someone was doing something I wanted to do but never got the chance to do out of fear!

I used to think, *What is wrong with me?* What was wrong with me was that I needed to sit down with myself, heal, and understand who I was in the Lord personally. It was never the other person; it was something deeper going on that I honestly had no clue of until I began to have intentional moments with myself. Seriously.

Even when getting into a relationship, there were times when I would begin to see those feelings arise, and I had to fight them off. When those thoughts came, I had to fight because I knew who I was, but I wanted to be someone for someone else to like me more. I felt like being myself was a problem.

Ladies, let me just tell you, **Please be so in love with god that when you begin to question your worth, you will know how to shut up the enemy and his lies, okay?**

Even if you are in high school or middle school, please take the time to embrace the girl/teen/young adult that you are now so that when you get older, you will not have any issues with fully walking in who you are unapologetically!

Seriously! Never allow someone to make you feel less than because you are not. If you ever begin to feel less than good enough or not enough, pick up your Word and begin to study about what and who God says you are!

You are the apple of his eye (Deuteronomy 32:10).[3]

You are fearfully and wonderfully made (Psalm 139:14).

You are enough (Isaiah 49:16).

You were chosen by him (1 Peter 2:9-17).!

You are seated in heavenly places with the Father (Ephesians 2:6).

You are forgiven (Psalm 32:1).

You are the daughter of a King (Psalm 45:9-11).

You are the Bride of Christ (Ephesians 5:22-23).

You are created in the image of God—"The Imago Dei" (Genesis 1:27).

Listen, sister, that's who you are! You are not your hair. You are not the clothes you wear—even though, honey, you are rocking those outfits! You are not the way your body is shaped. You are not the way your teeth are made. You are not the color of your skin. You are not what someone said to you back in elementary school. You are who God says you are! You rock her very well. Don't let the lies continue to tell you otherwise.

It's time to put on your flats, heels, or sneaks, and walk into your true, authentic self. If you want to, take out the weave. Take off the eyelashes. Take the makeup off. Take off every piece of jewelry. Take off everything and just look at yourself

---

[3] I have paraphrased the verses on this page so that they can speak directly to you.

in a full-length mirror. Do that! Honey, if you have to cry, then cry. If you have to just stare at yourself, then just stare. If you must turn around and look at yourself again, do that. But really embrace who you are, sister!

Now ask yourself, "What or who have I been comparing myself to and why?"

Take inventory of what you are doing and the names that have come to your mind. I had to write out names and forgive myself for putting myself down for doing this because there is no way on God's green earth we are supposed to be comparing ourselves to another sister in Christ.

By doing that, we are just telling God that He hasn't done a great job creating us when, in reality, He has done much better than great. Just as He did for me by setting me free from comparing myself to others, He will do the same thing for you if you let Him!

I'll let you in on a little secret to loving who you are and why He created you the way He did: You have to begin to embrace all of YOU. Will the past ever try to creep in? Yes, because you may have yet to deal with the root cause of everything! For me, it was so heavy that, at one point, I began to get depressed over the simple things. We will chat about that in the next chapter, as well!

Anywho, no one on this earth resembles you! (Even if you are a twin. You may look alike, but there are some differences between you.) Now, tell yourself that you are a beautiful woman. Your smile is contagious. Your hair is ahhh-mazing! Whether your hair is straight, curly, bald, low cut, low curly, bobbianna, shoulder length, long, whatever, **honey, you are beautiful!** (I've had to do this same thing.)

There were moments when I would stand in front of my mirror and hype myself up to embody the woman who God has made me into. Through everything that I have gone through, God still calls me beautiful and His. So are you! Embrace who He has created you to be.

More challenges in relationships came my way in adulthood because I lacked identity. When I say relationships, I mean friendships as well. Because I felt like I knew what I wanted, I just went with what I knew I wanted. I am being so transparent here because I know women are reading this who have fallen to a place before where they didn't want to be. A place where you felt your lowest. A place where the only escape route was not being here anymore. There were many times I was too afraid just to be myself authentically. I scaled back big time because I would worry about the opinions of others to the point that sometimes I was not fun to be around.

Sometimes, I would just sit back and thank God for where he has brought me from. When those comparing thoughts try to arise, **shut them up!** Yes, "shut up" is a very bad saying (this is what I tell my niece and nephew, anyway), but sometimes you have to get fed up with the enemy's tricks and begin to fight him back with positive things about yourself!

The back of this book contains some scriptures, along with where to read about them to build yourself up.

You can and will get through this, girl! Trust me. Sometimes, you may have to stay in one Saturday night and bask in the Lord's presence, learn to cook a new meal, or find yourself a new hobby you know you will love to do in your home. I tell you that in this season of my life, that is what I am on. It's such a beautiful thing, honestly. You've got this sis. I am cheering you on!

TIME OF REFLECTION!

(Grab your tea, coffee, bottled water, and a pen and journal, sister!)

1. What are some areas of your adult life where you aren't feeling your best self? Why? Is that from God or the enemy?
2. What is one new hobby that you can begin to do to see life differently? We don't have to always go out on a Saturday night, we can also have fun at our own place.
3. Do you believe that God can and will grow you from the area of comparison? Do you believe that it is just a spirit that's trying to hold you back from succeeding in life?

THE COMPARISON GAME

– CHAPTER 6 –

SOCIAL MEDIA, DEPRESSION, AND SUICIDE

"These things I have spoken to you, that in Me you may have peace. In the world you will have tribulation; but be of good cheer, I have overcome the world."
—John 16:33

Ladies, now you know I couldn't let this go by without breaking these main three topics down: social media, depression, and suicide. I have dealt with all three tremendously when comparing myself and feeling less than!

Whew, okay. In today's society, everyone has social media. Whether it's YouTube, TikTok, Instagram, Facebook, Twitter, Myspace, Snapchat, or LinkedIn, nearly everyone in today's society has at least one of these platforms. When I saw that my grandpa has a Facebook, I was like, "Oh geesh, yeah, literally everyone has one now." Ha-ha.

These platforms can be a massive cause for women comparing themselves today. There are so many things that say, "You're not small enough," "You're not thick enough," and "Oh, wait, I need your hair to be this way." "You're not light enough," or "You could be a little darker."

I need you to just be you!

Some spaces out there invite you to be yourself, but some people don't think that being their true authentic self will get them anywhere in life. Baby, that is a lie from the pit of hell!

I know for me... Whew, am I going to go there?

I mean, why not? Expose the enemy, right?

YEP!

Sometimes, I would scroll for hours on social media, looking at other people's lives as inspiration until I started to compare. I remembered a time when I compared myself to a certain sister in Christ. I said, "God, I don't want this spirit, and I am going to shine a light on what the enemy is trying to hide. No more hiding, Satan!"

I went and told her that I had started comparing myself to her. I didn't know what she would think when I told her; I just told her I wanted to be free. Once I got it out, I tell you the weight lifted off me! I said, "Wow, God, that was a burden I was carrying when I could've just released that thing a while back." Man, oh, man.

Sisters, sometimes you have to do what's uncomfortable to really begin to breathe and realize that you are not living the way you need to live (in freedom, not bondage). Sometimes, taking a break is necessary to clear your mind and focus on the things in front of you. **Take a mental break for yourself!**

I love taking breaks from social media. I've been off it since May 2023, and honestly, I haven't missed it. Friends ask me, "When are you getting back on?" I replied, "Girl, I have no idea."

There are things on social media that are good for you to tend to, but if you know that you will get on there and compare yourself to Kara, Susan, Casey, and Jasmine, then do yourself a favor and stay off, sis. It is so much better to heal and free yourself from the junk that's been hiding in you. Girl, get rid and stay free!

I learned that people only post what they want you to see. Most people do not post the ugly parts of their life. Now, to the ones who do, I salute you! It's so good and refreshing to see people be their authentic self! Would I always do that? No, until I got tired of trying to "Put On."

When I think about my social media, it was much about me and not much about Jesus. I wanted my page to be more aesthetically pleasing than helping others come to Christ by sharing my testimony. Nothing is wrong with a nice profile, but make sure you are being your authentic self. Now, will the enemy try? Heck yeah, he has no new tricks, but I will be stronger to fight this time, and so will you.

So, if you are scrolling and looking at other women's bodies, stop and look at yours. A woman who loves herself is a strong woman. Never give up on yourselves, ladies. I don't care what it takes. **Don't give up on you!**

Unfortunately, I know of many cases where women have given up on themselves for numerous reasons. Let's talk about it.

Depression is real.

May I say that again, **depression is real**. But you can overcome it. Of course, it's a spirit! It will speak louder to you than any other thought. I remember struggling with depression big time. There would be days when I would just want to lay in bed and do nothing. There were days when I would be quiet and, better yet, just cry. On those days, I didn't want to be with anyone or even talk. If you haven't noticed by now, I love to talk.

As I type this, all I want to do is cry because I can think back on a time recently when I was depressed, and I had to talk myself out of it. When you don't, those thoughts of not needing to be on this earth could come in—thoughts like, *I just need to end it; everyone would be so much better off without me; people just want from me, but no one really sees me*, or *no one wants me unless I do something for them.*

These thoughts can ruin your life. They can destroy relationships. They can even hinder so much from coming to you because all you hear are the loud negative thoughts in your ear instead of the voice of your Father.

The voice that's telling you to hold on.

The voice that's telling you, "I love you."

The voice that's telling you, "Don't do it. As long as you hold on, I have so much in store for you."

The voice that tells you, "I am proud of you regardless of your past."

The voice that tells you, "No matter what, you are mine."

The voice that says, "And I have grace for that, and for that, and for that every time you try to write yourself off."

That voice that will make you feel like you are seen by someone else.

No, you can't see Him, but if you look hard enough at the things around you, you can begin to see him, feel him, and hear him. When the negative thoughts are louder than the still, small ones, please take a deep breath and begin to say the name of Jesus.

JESUS! JESUS! JESUS! Demons tremble at the sound of his name!

Depression will not have you. The only medicine you need is the **word of God**. How do I know? I remember it like it was yesterday. I remember when I would be driving on the highway in Atlanta, and I would literally hear, "Drive yourself off the I-285 bridge," while going to Camp Creek. The thoughts were that loud. Seriously!

Then there was this one time when I was sitting in the bathroom, and I texted my family group chat to let them know how tired I was. Negative thoughts were overtaking me, and I didn't know what to do. I felt hopeless. It was a good thing I have a praying family, though. My aunt quickly texted me aside from the family group chat.

"Have you ever had suicidal thoughts?" she asked.

"Yes, ma'am," I texted back.

"Well, if you don't go and get help, I will send people to take you," she responded.

God, I don't need that, I thought while reading her message. *I just need to talk and get everything out.*

So, my cousin came down and took me to a behavioral hospital.

"Sis," she said. "I am coming down to be with you."

I remember her coming down and going with me to the facility. Sitting there, I listened to everyone's story and told myself, *This isn't me. I don't need to be here! I just need to talk to someone.*

They began to run tests to see what they could diagnose me with, but the doctor didn't find anything wrong.

"Um, ma'am, we don't see anything wrong with you," the doctor said. "There is nothing off balance."

"Ma'am, I know," I replied. "I am just here because I told my aunt I would come, and I didn't want her calling the police because she would."

She wasn't going to go through having her niece commit suicide when she could do something to stop it. Deep down, I began to get angry with myself because I knew this wasn't me. I knew this wasn't who my parents raised me to be. My thoughts just wouldn't let me live. They were constantly coming after me LOUD.

Being at this place where I never thought I would get to—a place of rock bottom. I remember being so afraid of what my family and friends would think, but I didn't care at that moment. I just wanted help, but the help I neglected was right in front of me the whole time. That was God. A true relationship with Him would've helped me escape what I was experiencing. I began to notice that there wasn't really anything wrong with me.

Why am I sharing this with you? I didn't go through this for no reason. That was in 2017, and since then, I have learned how to war differently. That experience showed me that this is a bigger fight. Depression and suicide are spiritual battles that you must fight!

You have the weapon to fight, so use it.

The suicide rate has gone up, and it breaks my heart. After reading so many things in the media about women committing suicide, my heart aches so badly.

I remember sitting on the edge of my bed in 2022, saying, "God, I have to write this book. I don't know whose life it will touch, but if I can just help one, that's who I am meant to help."

Ladies, suicide is not an option. It is what the enemy wants you to do! He knows that if we, as women, commit suicide and don't know whose we are, then how will we be able to reproduce into the world?! He wants you to think you don't have a life or that your life is so bad that it will never improve.

It can and will get better for you! There is no need to hurt yourself. If you didn't bring yourself into this world, you can't take yourself out of it. That is what I had to tell myself when I had those thoughts.

Please don't let anything get you to a point where you want to commit suicide. You are worth so much more than that. Jesus Christ died on the cross for you and everything you are dealing with.

Just read it in His Word. There are so many times when the Lord explains His love for you. The fact that Jesus walked this earth and was crucified on the cross—dying the worst death anyone could imagine—for you tells you that He knows how you feel. He understands when you want to give up, and He hears your tears. He wept (John 11:35).

He understands when things are going on in your life, and you wonder, "God, why me?" He gets it! He had a thorn crown beat into his head; he was whipped until all you saw was blood. He had nails hammered into his hands and feet. I mean, everything that you're feeling, he has felt!

Don't let the enemy punk you out because you aren't that!

You are a warrior. I am here today to let you know that you are more than a conqueror. You are an overcomer, and you will overcome these problems! That's right. You will overcome these problems. God is not done with you yet. He has written your life from beginning to end. He formed you in your mother's womb, so you must know that He knows when you will leave this earth and how. But the enemy also has a plan. Whose will you follow? The King of Kings and Lord of Lords or the enemy? Choose this day whom you will serve.

God has your back, sister. He has your back! (I am literally stretching mine right now, and it feels so good).

Suicide is not the answer, and if you are dealing with that today, I am here to let you know you are going to win this battle. *The enemy will not have you.* Point blank, period. That's it, that's all. Write out your biblical affirmations that tell you what the Word says you are. Then, do what you have to do to become set free.

The spirit of comparison is one ugly, rude, nasty spirit. As the apostle Paul wrote in 2 Corinthians 10:12, "For we dare not class ourselves or compare ourselves with those who commend themselves. But they, measuring themselves by themselves and comparing themselves among themselves, are not wise." So you shouldn't compare. You are a unique individual. God made you with your uniqueness because there is something on this earth that only you can fulfill. If you resist the enemy and give God your life, God will begin to unfold so many things to you, one by one. Now, He is not going to show you everything at once. He doesn't want to overwhelm you. Remember, this is not a race. God doesn't mind going at your pace. He wants to walk with you through this. He has your back; remember that! Also, remember you aren't going through what you're going through for any reason. It's for someone else. What I mean when I say this is that your testimony is to help others who are lost get free! We are here to be the light to the earth! Yes, it may seem a bit much, but count it all joy; suffering won't always last!

TIME OF REFLECTION!

(Grab your tea, coffee, bottled water, and a pen and journal, sister!)

1. What are some things that you do when you scroll on social media? Are they healthy for you? Be honest with yourself. Ask the Holy Spirit.
2. Can you name a time when you were depressed? What was the situation? How did you overcome it? What can you do next time to prevent this from happening?
3. Do you think suicide will solve your problem? If so, why? If you chose to fight regardless of how you're feeling, imagine how the victory would be on the other side of what you are going through.

THE COMPARISON GAME

— CHAPTER 7 —

AFTER THE STORM COMES A RAINBOW!

"Every good gift and every perfect gift is from above, and comes down from the Father of lights, with whom there is no variation or shadow of turning."
—James 1:17

It is not always easy to understand how much the Lord loves you. When in the wilderness, it's especially hard to believe that God is with you. One thing I can tell you is that if you are currently going through a wilderness season, begin to speak life into that season no matter what it looks like on the outside.

Speak power over yourself.
Speak healing to the situation.
Command things to shift.
If you didn't know, your words have so much power!
That's why it is essential to watch what you say, **always**! As it says in the Bible, "Death and Life are in the power of the tongue ..." (Proverbs 18:21). I would hear that, but I didn't believe it until I began to see some things I said come to pass in my life. There's grace for you. There's mercy for you. Never give up! Now, as you go through life, remember what

the Lord says. Remember how he loves. Remember how he carries you—day in and day out.

Throughout your life, you may have had to be the strong one. Maybe you were the one who had to keep your family together because of not-so-good circumstances. Things in your life have happened to you for a reason. No, they may not have been the best things at all times, but they grew, matured, and got you in such a space to know that no one but the Lord was there guiding and keeping you through it all. The title of this chapter is literally true. There may be many storms in your life, even at this moment when you are reading this book. I want you to know that there is a rainbow coming really soon. Where did the rainbow originate from? Let's go back to Genesis 6 regarding Noah and the Ark.

"Then the Lord saw that the wickedness of man was great in the earth, and that every intent of the thoughts of his heart was only evil continually. And the Lord was sorry that He made man on the earth, and He was grieved in His heart. So the Lord said, 'I will destroy man whom I have created from the face of the earth, both man and beast, creeping thing and birds of the air, for I am sorry that I have made them.' But Noah found grace in the eyes of the Lord" (Genesis 6:5-8).

So the Lord spoke and told Noah to grab seven each of every clean animal, a male and his female; two each of animals that are unclean, a male and his female; also seven each of birds of the air, male and female, to keep the species alive on the face of all the earth.

Then, the Lord told Noah that he would make a covenant with him. He was going to bring a flood onto the earth to wipe away every living creature. So, Noah followed the instructions from the Lord and brought every living thing onto the boat. They were in the boat for 40 days and 40 nights.

During this time, the Lord remembered Noah. He began to dry up the land day by day until there was no more water on the earth. Once there wasn't any more flooding, the Lord made a covenant with Noah:

"Thus I establish My covenant with you: Never again shall all flesh be cut off by the waters of the flood; never again shall there be a flood to destroy the earth." And God said: 'This is the sign of the covenant which I make between Me and you, and every living creature that is with you, for perpetual generations: I set My rainbow in the cloud, and it shall be for the sign of the covenant between Me and the earth.'" (Genesis 9:11-13).

Noah knew that the covenant remained because a rainbow appeared in the sky. Well, ladies, what do you see in the sky today after it rains? A rainbow! So, the covenant still remains.

When I first read this, I thought, *Wait a minute, God. You said that you will not bring a flood on the earth anymore to wipe away all humanity, but what about the floods that happen today in some major cities?*

He told me to look closer at the scripture. He said he wouldn't send a flood to wipe away ALL of humanity. I said, "Oh, wow! Okay, Holy Spirit, thank you!"

See, sister, the storm may last a very long time in your eyes, but just hold on. Trust that God has you in the palm of his hands, and He knows exactly what He is doing. Seriously! He knows exactly how you feel, but remember that you will get through this one day at a time. Just trust the process with the Lord.

When you begin to feel a certain way about yourself, just look into scripture and remind yourself what the Lord says about you! Never give up on you. If the Lord hasn't given up on you, and He woke you up today, trust that He still has a plan for your life. He has given you breath for another day, so there is something on this earth for you to do, and only **you can do it!**

Don't give the enemy an inch because he will take a foothold (Ephesians 4:27). Listen to the Lord in this season of your life. Stay away from anything that can and will send you backward. If you don't fit in anymore, that's good because that means you're growing. If you're doing different things that you've never done before, that's good too because you're beginning to live your life for you.

WELCOME TO THE SOUND OF FREEDOM

I will share where I am right now in my life. There was always an inkling of knowing that one state was not my end all be all. I knew the Lord would move me; I just didn't know when He would move me. It happened a few years ago when I was fed up with life and wanted to move.

"God, can I go?" "Can I leave Georgia, and will you be with me when I go?"

According to Hebrews 13:5, "Let your conduct be without covetousness; be content with such things as you have. For He Himself has said, 'I will never leave you nor forsake you.'"

Honestly, I was afraid to move. My motives back then weren't good. I wanted to run from my problems: the low self-esteem, the internal battle, the comparison, the lack of feeling loved, I mean, you name it.

Mentally, I was going through a war I didn't want to fight, and I thought leaving would fix it. Instead of facing it, I just wanted to take cover and hide.

Remember, don't run from your problems; face them head-on. God is with you in the fight. He is fighting on your behalf! I thought moving away would be better for me and everyone, and I just wanted to get away from the mistakes I had made. I wanted to run and experience life in a new state with new scenery, people, and everything.

I was about to leave, but I didn't. I couldn't. I had more growing to do. I decided to give Georgia another shot. As I write this, I am amazed at what God has done and how he has moved me. If I had moved then, who knows where I would've been? I truly thank God for where I am today.

This new season of freedom didn't come easy. There were many, many, many trials that I had to go through. I did not know who I was in the kingdom of God, and I allowed myself to respond out of fear. I was lukewarm—point blank—until I began to say, "Enough is enough." I had to be intentional about receiving my freedom and staying free.

You know there are times you can get free and then allow the enemy's tricks to come back and now you're in the cycle all over again? I am going to be so honest here—there were many cycles that I kept getting into. I couldn't get it, and I couldn't catch a break. But God! The woman I am today had to endure many, many things that were not pleasant, from having my real father tell me he wasn't my father (even though he knew he was) to feeling so little and like no one would want me.

Well, I am here to tell you: Sister, someone wants me—and he wants you too! He is the most perfect man there is. And who is that? Jesus Christ!

Whew! I am so thankful to be a daughter of a King. He is the King of Kings and the Lord of Lords! Just think about that for a moment. Let me tell you, whatever you may be dealing with right now, get through it. Do not dwell in that place. I did a lot of dwelling, which brought me nothing but restless nights. Lay your problems at the feet of Jesus. He desires intimacy with you. He desires more of you than just going to him with your problems. He wants your entire life. He wants to guide the boat for you.

Living now in another state, I am in awe of what the Lord has done thus far. It's all because I have finally decided to let my feelings and everything else go out the window. I have a good friend who always says, "Girl, killing your flesh is a daily thing. Those feelings are feelings, but what is the root cause?!"

When I tell you it is good to have a good circle around you, it is. Those who will call you out in love when you're not acting right, those who pray for you and with you and not against you, those who really love you for you, and most importantly, those who will lead you to Jesus and not just their opinions. Check your circle as you are growing with God. It's good to have those people in your corner who will walk through a drought season of your life while still encouraging you to be your best self. Be honest with people and yourself. You will save a lot of heartache and sleepless nights if you are honest with people from the beginning.

God knows you better than you know yourself. Why not let him be the one who controls it? There may be moments when you feel alone and begin to get in your thoughts about who you are as a woman. Let me tell you, don't do that! That is the quickest way to get so far behind because you're allowing those things to come back and creep into your life when the Lord has already freed you. Stay free, and live for God fully!

Also, do not continue to look back at your past. Yes, your past is what made you into the woman you are today, but do not think of your past and allow shame and condemnation to creep into you. That is not of the Lord! Your past is in the past for a reason. You had to grow through some things to better understand the Love of Our Father.

Listen, we don't deserve him. Apostle Paul said, "For all have sinned and fall short of the Glory of God" (Romans 3:23), but that doesn't mean He loves you any less. He wants you to change your ways, turn from them, and *follow Him*! That's it, that's all. You can and will overcome anything if you just continue to pursue God. He is right by your side.

I know that this book is about you not comparing yourself, but I just had to encourage you as well because we live in a day where there is an enemy that's out to sift you as wheat (Luke 22:31), and if you are not strong in the Lord, you will be sifted out! Stay strong and stand tall in the Lord and what He is doing in your life.

Remember your life is not about you. Let me say that again: **your life is not about you.** We are here to do the will of Our Father. I say that because, in today's world, people are all about me, me, me (i.e., what can I do to get this or what can I do to get that because I want it).

Well, if God told you today to leave everything you put before him, will you do it? Your life is about being a disciple of the Lord, whether in the workplace, on the streets, or in the shopping store.

Recently, I have begun to tell myself that even with my job, I am working unto my Father. He is the one who gave me this job, so I will steward this job well. I will show up on time. I will be truthful. I will be kind, and I will love on those who He sends my way.

Now, did I always do this? No, not one bit. It was tough for me to show up on time for work until I got this revelation. Living only five minutes from the airport, I knew I would show up on time, but because I didn't check my email concerning the new bus route due to construction, I would be a tad bit late. See, it's the little things that matter the most, like checking an email.

Honestly, that's not acceptable. Even showing up to church late on a Sunday is not acceptable. Why would we arrive late to the House of the Lord but try to get to work on time? No, if we are going to work on our character and be on time in one area, let's begin to be on time all the way around. Okay, okay, I'll leave that there.

So, sister, if you haven't gotten anything else from this book, one thing I want to leave with you is that you are who you are in the eyes of the Lord. Do not allow the world to tell you who you are. You are not your accolades. You are who the Lord designed you to be. There is a song called "You Can Have It All" by Mercy Culture Worship. When I first heard this song, it resonated with my spirit so much because it literally all belongs to the Lord!

The song states, "It will never be mine! It will always be yours," which is so true. None of the things we have are ours. We are just stewards of the things the Lord has given us. Literally. There are many things that I am thinking of at this moment that are not mine but my Father's. So, that issue that happened to you in the past belongs to the Father. Give it to him. Give up the control and let the Lord fill you up with his love anyway! You don't have the energy to continue to hold onto it. Don't you want to see how life would be if you forgave the person who did you wrong?

Honey, forgive and move on. Seriously! It is not for the other person. They are sound asleep at night while you are the one tossing and turning, wondering why you are not sleeping well. I am here to tell you to FORGIVE. Jesus even states in the Word that we are supposed to forgive seventy times seven (Matthew 18:21), which means we are supposed to forgive continuously. Work on forgiving day and night. If you must write it out to remember, then do that. Write it anywhere that you can see it daily, and trust that the Lord will begin to work on your heart to release the emotion attached to forgiveness.

One part of "You Can Have It All," goes, "Our status, our names, our titles, our fame, we lay down our crowns" Listen, lay it all down at the feet of the Father. It all belongs to Him. He can have it all. Submit yourself to the Father and His will for your life. Acknowledge whatever you need to and let the Father do what he needs to do to clean you up and heal you!

You will get through this, and remember that you don't have to play the comparison game because He didn't create you for that. He created you for his ultimate game, winning souls for the Kingdom of God!

— CHAPTER 8 —

THE NEW BEGINNING ... COMPARING YOURSELF TO JESUS!

> "For with God nothing will be impossible."
> —Luke 1:37

As I wrote this book, I thought it was finished after chapter 7, but the thing is, it wasn't. As I was leaving work one day, the Lord spoke to me about this chapter through a bus driver, then through a dear friend, and then again to me. This new beginning involves surrendering everything, picking up your cross, and following Jesus.

What do we define as a New Beginning? Well, some may say that a new beginning is starting over. Whether that's moving to a new state, getting a new job, owning a home, I mean, you name it. All of these things can be defined as what someone would say a new beginning is for them, but if your mind isn't renewed from your past, is it really a new beginning?

You can be in a new space, have a new job, or move to a different state and still be stuck in the past. So, what does this new beginning consist of?

Well, it consists of you having the mind of Christ and being a disciple for Him! As it states in Mark 8:34, "When He had called the people to Himself, with His disciples also, He said to them, 'Whoever desires to come after Me, let him deny himself, and take up his cross, and follow me!'" Following Christ means leaving the old behind and truly following what He says. Following the direction He tells you to go. Think the way He does, and respond the way He wants you to respond.

This new beginning may be what you need, but you don't know how to get to it without trying to hold onto what was.

Let it go. The Bible states in Luke 14:27, "And whoever does not bear his cross and come after Me cannot be My disciple." I know how it feels to do things I wanted to do and not have a personal relationship with the Father to hear exactly what He wanted from me.

Living life the way I wanted had me looking at life through the lens of the world. Seeing life through the lens of the world will leave you empty inside. You want everything that the world says is good instead of asking the Father what He desires for you to have.

In the Word, it states that we have an inheritance. We are descendants of Abraham. So everything that the Father told Abraham and then to Issac is ours! At this point in your life, you may have everything you want, but you may still be empty inside. The things of this world shouldn't satisfy you; only God should!

I have had trouble with this in my life. I wanted everything I saw instead of being content with where God had me and trusting that whatever He wanted for me, I would have, just in His timing.

Having everything in the world but not having a truly intimate relationship with the One who created you will still have you striving for more of what the world can give instead of thriving in what the Lord has given!

Have you taken a second to ask God what is in your hand? The Lord has placed something special in your hand, and He has gifted you to do the very thing He has given you! Trust in your capability to do what the Lord has set before you!

By having the mind of Christ, you are no longer comparing yourself to the world and what the world does or has. So, let's rejoice that you will no longer compare yourself to anything or anyone else but simply compare yourself to the one who created you! This is the New Beginning!

"If then you were raised with Christ, seek those things which are above, where Christ is, sitting at the right hand of God. Set your mind on things above, not on things on the earth. For you died, and your life is hidden with Christ in God. When Christ who is our life appears, then you also will appear with Him in glory. Therefore put to death your members which are on the earth: fornication, unclean news, passion, evil desire, and covetousness, which is idolatry. Because of these things the wrath of God is coming upon the sons of disobedience, in which you yourselves once walked when you lived in them. But now you yourselves are to put off all these: anger, wrath, malice, blasphemy, filthy language out of your mouth. Do not lie to one another, since you have put off the old man with his deeds, and have put on the new man who is renewed in knowledge according to the image of Him who created him, where there is neither Greek nor Jew, circumcised nor uncircumcised, barbarian, Scythian, slave nor free, but Christ is all and in all" (Colossians 3:1-11).

Since we now have the mind of Christ and we're comparing ourselves to Jesus, we should carry ourselves according to the Word of God. Yes, this can be challenging at times, but if we invite the Holy Spirit into our day-to-day lives, He will show us the way. He is so close when we invite Him into it.

This new mind will have you leave the past in the past and really begin to focus on what the Lord wants instead of what you want! Being in a place where you let go of everything and desire what the Lord desires. In this space, ask the Father to give you a heart that hates what He hates and loves what He loves!

"Therefore, as the elect of God, holy and beloved, put on tender mercies, kindness, humility, meekness, long suffering; bearing with one another, and forgiving one another if anyone has a complaint against another; even as Christ forgave you, so you also must do. But above all these things put on love, which is the bond of perfection. And let the peace of God rule in your hearts, to which also you were called in one body; and be thankful. Let the word of Christ dwell in you richly in all wisdom, teaching and admonishing one another in psalms and hymns and spiritual songs, singing with grace in your hearts to the Lord. And whatever you do in word or deed, do all in the name of the Lord Jesus, giving thanks to the Father through Him" (Colossians 3:12-17).

This scripture speaks very loudly on what the Father wants us to do. When I looked up this scripture, I saw that the title of this section is The Character of the New Man. This scripture tells us to carry the Fruit of the Spirit and be like Christ. We are to be kind to one another even in the midst of adversity. We are to walk around with humility, understanding that we are just a vessel of the Lord. It's not about the titles or the fame but about bringing other people to realize who the Father is! It's about being a disciple of Christ!

There's long-suffering, which I can attest to. Long-suffering is never a good feeling. Not understanding how to manage what the Father gives you can be one thing, but then again, going in a repetitive cycle because you don't have a true relationship with the Father is what keeps you in the cycle. It is important to have a personal relationship with God. You need to understand what the Father is doing and how He moves on your behalf!

"He must increase, but I must decrease" (John 3:30). This scripture explains it all. As Jesus increases in our lives, we must take it upon ourselves to decrease in everything around us.

This scripture tells me that no matter what situation may come my way, I must respond the way Christ would. Since putting Jesus first and myself second, I have seen a drastic change in my walk with Him. I was once a person who really liked to have control over situations. I would think about the best plan I thought was right instead of seeking the Father's thoughts on the situation.

Once I released the want to have control, I saw Jesus come in and transform me from the inside out. Did it happen overnight? No, it didn't, but there were things that I definitely saw drastically change in my life, and I am forever grateful for that.

Remember that you can say Yes to Jesus anytime! Yes to His will, and Yes to His way, which is the best way. What does comparing yourself to Christ look like? Reform your mind to have the mind of Christ. Our mind is very powerful. Our mind and our heart are connected.

According to Webster's dictionary, reform means to put or change into an improved form or condition, as well as to put an end to (an evil) by enforcing or introducing a better method or course of action. So, not only are you reforming your mind, but you are also reforming your heart. This looks like asking the Father to search you and make every crooked path straight in your mind and heart.

The Lord is so close to the brokenhearted. You are dealing with things that the Lord can and will heal. Again, He must increase in your life, but you **must decrease** (JOHN 3:30). To have a reformed mind, you must be intentional about spending time daily with the Father who loves you so much. Encounter Him daily to understand how to reform your mind. Allow the Father to fill you up to remind you of who you are in Him and who He is in **every situation** of your life.

"Then Jesus said to His disciples, 'If anyone desires to come after Me, let him deny himself, and take up his cross, and follow Me. For whoever desires to save his life will lose it, but whoever loses his life for My sake will find it'" (Matthew 16:24-25).

Listen, your life is not about you! I had to understand this for myself. Yes, we are here to do the will of Our Father. Still, at the end of the day, we must die to ourselves daily and understand that every single thing that we go through in life, wait, I don't like to say it that way, every single thing that we GROW through in life is for us to share our testimony with someone else who may be going through a similar season as OURS.

During the testing and trials, trust me, it didn't feel good. I have been in many incidents where the trial seemed unbearable to GROW through at the time, but on the other side of the trial, I can say that I am thankful that I went through it because I had to learn so much about myself and grow into the woman that I am today! Taking up our cross can be challenging at times, but it is so worth it to live the life the Lord has for us!

"Yea, though I walk through the valley of the shadow of death, I will fear no evil; For You are with me; Your rod and Your staff, they comfort me" (Psalm 23:4).

Throughout my life, fear stifled me from doing some of the things I really wanted to do. Now, thinking how the Father wants me to think, I must put on the helmet of salvation and blot out the spirit of fear that tries to come in throughout my day-to-day life. I was a person who listened to the news just to hear the bad news and then dwell on what was going on in the world. Let's just say this isn't a good thing because as you try to surrender everything to the Father, you must silence the voices telling you otherwise about the world and even yourself.

Keeping your mind on things above and not on things on this earth is the most important thing to do in this walk with the Father. Remember to surround your thoughts with things from the Bible and His commandments instead of wondering about the things of this life because they will all fade away one day. We are here for such a time, and while we are here, we must fear **only the Lord**. This goes into the scripture: We shouldn't fear the one who can harm the body but not the soul, but we should fear the one who can harm both body and soul!

"Finally, brethren, whatever things are true, whatever things are noble, whatever things are just, whatever things are pure, whatever things are lovely, whatever things are of good report, if there is any virtue and if there is anything praiseworthy—meditate on these things. The things which you learned and received and heard and saw in me, these do, and the God of peace will be with you" (Philippians 4:8).

I remember having to quote this scripture repeatedly because the thoughts going through my head were louder than the voice of God. Having the mind of Christ, we must understand that we are to think like Christ thought!

Think about things that are above, even in the midst of a storm. There will be moments in life where the enemy will try to come up to cause chaos in your life, but you must remember who is in control and who is the one who knows your beginning to end. Don't give in to the temptations of the enemy. That's what He wants you to do.

Before I understood the authority I have in Christ, I would think about things that are negative all the time. I would think the worst before thinking positively, and that didn't get me anywhere in life but stagnant. Now, understanding the works of the enemy, I can sit and dwell on the negative or meditate on what I know is true, which is the Word of God!

We are overcome by the blood of the Lamb and by the word of our testimony! You must go and testify about the goodness of the Lord. Once lost and now found, many others are where you once were. I can relate to this new beginning of life and having the mind of Christ.

Many times in my earlier years, I would believe the lie of what the enemy would tell me. I wanted to give up, and I put the enemy (without even realizing it) above God because I would worry about everything instead of worship. I kept things to myself because I thought that was best, but in reality, it wasn't. It hurt me more than anything because I was holding onto things that burdened me instead of releasing them and giving them to the Father.

One thing I had to do was renew my mind. It was the one thing that was getting in the way of so many things occurring in my life. I decided to give God my all and release the control over my life. When you have control over your life, you are not letting God be God. You are putting him in a box that He doesn't belong in. Don't put Him in a box! He is bigger than your problems!

When you release control, invite the Father into your life, and listen, you will see things change for the better. There were many nights when I had to war and renounce the lies the enemy told me. The enemy knows how to get to you! He knows how to keep you stagnant. Don't let him have that much power over you. He is so small compared to our God!

After renouncing the lies and combating them with the Word of God, you must remain in truth and stand firm on what you know is true. Now, this doesn't mean that the enemy won't try to attack you with the thoughts again, but now, because you know how to combat them, you will respond differently. Respond the way Christ would want you to respond.

You must fight differently with your renewed mind. "Repay no one evil for evil. Have regard for good things in the sight of all men. If your enemy is hungry, feed him; If he is thirsty, give him a drink; For in so doing you will heap coals of fire on his head. Do not be overcome by evil, but overcome evil with good" (Romans 12:17 & 20-21). Knowing this will help you to remember that no matter what is said or done to you, you will respond with the character of Jesus. You will respond in spirit and in truth. Understand that now you are a new creature in Christ. It is no longer you who lives, but your Father who lives in you!

SISTER:
You are loved.
You are valuable.
You are chosen.
You are enough.
You are more than a conqueror; you are an overcomer..

You are fearfully and wonderfully made.
You are powerful.
You are a friend of jesus.
You are a daughter of a king.
You are the bride of christ.

You are who you are and the Lord loves the way He created you because He created you for such a time as this.

I love you, sister. You have won the game!

WRITE A PERSONAL LOVE LETTER TO GOD

Sincerely,

H ey, sis, here are a few scriptures to meditate on to remind you of our Father's love for you![4]

FEAR:

- Proverbs 31:30: "Charm is deceitful and beauty is passing, But a woman who fears the LORD, she shall be praised."
- Isaiah 41:10: "Fear not, for I am with you; Be not dismayed, for I am your God. I will strengthen you, Yes, I will help you, I will uphold you with My righteous right hand."
- Matthew 10:28: "And do not fear those who kill the body but cannot kill the soul. But rather fear Him who is able to destroy both soul and body in hell."
- 1 John 4:18: "There is no fear in love; but perfect love casts out fear, because fear involves torment. But he who fears has not been made perfect in love."

FORGIVENESS:

- Luke 17:3-4: "Take heed to yourselves. If your brother sins against you, rebuke him; and if he repents, forgive him. And if he sins against you seven times in a day, and seven times in a day returns to you, saying, 'I repent,' you shall forgive him."

---

4   All verses are from the NKJV.

- Ephesians 4:32: "And be kind to one another, tenderhearted, forgiving one another, even as God in Christ forgave you."
- Colossians 3:12-13: "Therefore, as the elect of God, holy and beloved, put on tender mercies, kindness, humility, meekness, longsuffering; bearing with one another, and forgiving one another, if anyone has a complaint against another; even as Christ forgave you, so you must do."
- Ephesians 1:7-10: "In Him we have redemption through His blood, the forgiveness of sins, according to the riches of His grace which He made to abound toward us in all wisdom and prudence, having made known to us the mystery of His will, according to His good pleasure which He purposed in Himself, that in the dispensation of the fullness of the times He might gather together in one all things in Christ, both which are in heaven and which are on earth—in Him."

CHOSEN:

- Isaiah 43:10: "'You are My witnesses,'" says the Lord, 'And My servant whom I have chosen, that you may know and believe Me, and understand that I am He. Before Me there was no God formed, nor shall there be after Me.'"
- 1 Corinthians 1:27: "But God has chosen the foolish things of the world to put to shame the wise, and God has chosen the weak things of the world to put to shame the things which are mighty."
- Ephesians 1:4-5: "Just as he chose us in Him before the foundation of the world that we should be holy

and without blame before Him in love, having predestined us to the adoption as sons by Jesus Christ to Himself according to the good pleasure of His will."
- John 15:16: "You did not choose Me, but I chose you and appointed you that you should go and bear fruit, and that your fruit should remain, that whatever you ask the Father in My name He may give you."

LOVE:

- Leviticus 19:18: "You shall not take vengeance, nor bear any grudge against the children of your people, but you shall love your neighbor as yourself: I am the Lord."
- Matthew 5:44: "But I say to you, love your enemies, bless those who curse you, do good to those who hate you, and pray for those who spitefully use you and persecute you."
- Proverbs 10:12: "Hatred stirs up strife, But love covers all sins."
- 1 Timothy 1:5: "Now the purpose of the commandment is love from a pure heart, from a good conscience, and from sincere faith."

SHAME:

- Joel 2:26: "You shall eat in plenty and be satisfied, And praise the name of the Lord your God, Who has dealt wondrously with you; And My people shall never be put to shame."
- 1 Corinthians 1:27: "But God has chosen the foolish things of the world to put to shame the wise, and

God has chosen the weak things of the world to put to shame the things which are mighty."
- Philippians 3:19: "Whose end is destruction, whose god is their belly, and whose glory is in their shame—who set their mind on earthly things."
- Psalm 31:1: "In You, O Lord I put my trust; Let me never be ashamed; Deliver me in Your righteousness."

BEAUTIFUL:

- 1 Peter 3:3-4: "Do not let your adornment be merely outward—arranging the hair wearing gold, or putting on fine apparel—rather let it be the hidden person of the heart with the incorruptible beauty of a gentle and quiet spirit, which is very precious in the sight of God."
- Genesis 1:27: "So God created man in His own image; in the image of God He created him; male and female He created them."
- Psalm 139:14: "I will praise You, for I am fearfully and wonderfully made; marvelous are Your works, and that my soul knows very well."
- Proverbs 3:15-18: "She is more precious than rubies, and all the things you may desire cannot compare with her. Length of days is in her right hand, in her left hand riches and honor. Her ways are ways of pleasantness, and all her paths are peace. She is a tree of life to those who take hold of her, and happy are all who retain her."

ACKNOWLEDGMENTS

I would like to take the time to acknowledge everyone who played a part in helping me get through this book. From the prayers to the long, drawn-out phone conversations, listening to me cry about how I didn't know if I would be able to finish, I thank you all truly!

First, I have to thank my Lord and Savior, Jesus Christ, for helping me complete the book.

From my sisters, Verronica and Shanterria, to my friends, you know who you are. I wouldn't have been able to get through this book without the constant encouragement from my peers!

Thank you to my sweet friend Danielle for taking the time to go through the book chapter by chapter with me to help me get a running start on the editing process. Thank you for always speaking life into me and helping me understand that something bigger is at hand! Reminding me of the Father's love for me and that I have a voice and a story that would help so many who are experiencing the same things I have gone through. I clearly didn't know what I was doing. Thank you for the constant push to be my best self no matter the circumstances I may have encountered.

Thank you to my editor, Mary Rembert! I truly thank you for being there through the thick of the edits! Thank you for reminding me that I didn't have to rush the process. Thank you for making sure the book is what it is today! Your constant encouragement to dig deeper even when it didn't feel good to dig deep! You may not understand what you were doing for me, but you were having me go to a place where I was afraid to go but needed to! I am truly grateful to you! You've helped me in so many areas of my life just by your comments and encouragement. Thank you!

Thank you to Victory World Church in Atlanta, Georgia, for making me the leader I am.

Thank you to Worship With Wonders in Atlanta, Georgia, for teaching me how to be bold in the Lord without being afraid.

Finally, thank you to Mercy Culture in Dallas, Texas, for showing me what it looks like to embody the characteristics of Jesus Christ.

ABOUT THE AUTHOR

Kiarra Nesbit is a passionate author with a huge heart for the younger generation. Going through challenging mental, emotional, and relational trials in her early life, Kiarra is now committed to exposing the depths of where it all starts— identity.

As a huge advocate for God, her love for Jesus Christ always takes center stage. She knows that without Him, the little girl from Lumber City, Georgia, wouldn't be where she is today. She lives by the scripture, "For God has not given us a spirit of fear, but of power and of love and of a sound mind"*(*2 Timothy 1:7*)*.

In her spare time, Kiarra loves to decorate, thrift, create, and attend sporting events. *The Comparison Game* is her first book and will be the first of many!

Made in the USA
Middletown, DE
10 February 2025

70763448R00073